Queen Esther Alday Drake
1879 - 1936

Also by John W. Bates

Campfire Tales from the Exodus (2015)

Stewardship, Economics and Entropy (2015)

The Seventh Child: Memoir of John E. Drake 1879-1964 (2011)

Bringing the Apocrapha Out of the Closet (2010)

The Ancestry and Lineage of G. Walter Bates [1883-1970] and Sarah Ann Armistead Bates [1885-1974] (2006)

A Study of Demand for Transit Use (1981)

Also by Robin E. Bates

Shakespeare and the Cultural Colonization of Ireland (2008)

Queen Esther Alday Drake

(1879-1936)

and the Royal Ancestry of the

Alday Family of Southwest Georgia

By

John W. Bates

and

Robin E. Bates

Table of Contents

Preface

by John W. Bates

Queen Esther Alday Drake was my grandmother, but I never knew her. She died in 1936 and I was not born, the second son of her youngest daughter, until 1939. By the time I was born my grandfather, John E. Drake, had remarried and his second wife, Glennie Barber Sapp Drake, was the only maternal grandmother I knew. Everyone who did know Esther, or "Quinester" as many called her, spoke of her highly and with great affection.

In 2011 I finished editing the memoir written by my grandfather, John E. Drake[1], supplementing the family history included in that memoir with some additional research drawing significantly from a previous work by a distant family member[2]. In addition, I included a section with a small amount of history for the family of his first wife Queen Esther Alday Drake. That effort was limited by the amount of research material available to me at the time and by a desire to finish the Drake history, which was the primary work undertaken.

---

[1]The Seventh Child: Memoir of John E. Drake, 1879-1964. Edited and Additional Material by John W. Bates. CreateSpace Independent Publishing Platform, 2011

[2]Descendants of Exum Drake, Volume IV. Descendants of Exum Drake, Jr. Through Jenkins James Drake. Robert Eldon Drake, MD. Orlando Florida. 1978.

In the intervening years the resources for genealogical research have multiplied and internet sources, especially *Ancestry.com®*, have proliferated. With these new resources and with some hints, especially findings from the research performed by my daughter, Dr. Robin E. Bates, we have found new information and are able to address more definitely some questions and possible myths of family history and, perhaps, to add to them.

The intent here is to reproduce, with appropriate modifications, the Alday material included in the earlier work. That is the first chapter. This will be followed by commentary on the original material and additional ancestral information collected largely by Dr. Robin E. Bates, who has strong academic credentials in English literature and history as well as interests family genealogy. Thanks to her familiarity with the names of historical characters in Shakespeare's history plays and with those character's family members, a strong argument may be made that Queen Esther, probably named for the Biblical character, is of royal British (and Scots) descent, along with most if not all of the Alday family of southwest Georgia.

The Alday family has a long history in southwest Georgia, and has made significant contribution to the area. The family name is not widely known, except for one extremely unfortunate incident when six members of the Alday family were brutalized and slain by escaped convicts in rural

Seminole County in May, 1973.[3]

In English history there was a class of people below the "gentry" but who were independent landowners and who could be counted on for home defense where they generally served in the role of noncommissioned officers below sergeant. The appellation has been more recently used to describe a group without pretensions and who are stable, reliable citizens. My impression of the Aldays in Southwest Georgia is that they are a "yeomanry" in the modern world.

Even without pretensions, however, it is gratifying to think that perhaps one's family has some importance in history. Why else the growing interest in genealogy evidenced by the advertising campaigns for and apparent significant usage of on-line family history research sites. In 1950 novelist Thomas B. Costain published a work entitled "Son of a Hundred Kings". The title was based on a quotation used in the introduction to the work "Son of butcher, son of a baker, son of a hundred kings."[4] This is a good meme for anyone who might become too infatuated with whom their ancestors were. Certainly this research is not sufficient to claim royal titles, or preferential treatments. It is sufficient however, to exclaim: Wow, isn't that neat!

---

[3]Information about this event may be found by online search for "Alday Murders". Ned Alday, oldest of those slain, was a grandson of the younger brother of Queen Esther's father.

[4] the author of which I cannot locate, nor have I located a copy of the book for sourcing and verification

The Ancestry and Lineage in North America of Queen Esther Alday: 1879 - 1936[5]

The origins of the Alday family of southwest Georgia were not clear. There are at least two versions. A published version included in a history of Seminole County, Georgia, traces the family from England, settling first in Virginia with Josiah Alday locating in Burke County, Georgia, during the 1760's. A son, Benjamin Alday, and his wife Rhoda reportedly lived in Wilkinson County, Georgia then relocated to Butler County, Alabama, where Benjamin died. Rhoda and "several sons" then moved to Mitchell County, Georgia. This account lists three sons, one unnamed who relocated to Texas, Daniel and Littlebury (or Little Berry), both of whom settled in the Spring Creek area of what is now Seminole County, Georgia. Littlebury Alday was the grandfather of Queen Esther Alday, wife of John Eager Drake.

Another, more fanciful account also included in the genealogical collection of the Seminole County Library[6] relates a story claiming Alday family descent from an Irish immigrant called "Red", "Redman", or "Redmund" O'day. This narrative reports that in 1788, in the area near what is now Chattanooga, Tennessee, O'Day married a half Cherokee named

---

[4] Extracted from *The Seventh Child: Memoir of John E. Drake 1879 - 1964 (2011)* by John W. Bates.

[5] A copy of that typescript in included in the next chapter.

"Rain Deer" and had a son who was named "Rain" or later "Ryan" O'Day. Ryan O'Day reportedly relocated to Baker County, Georgia,b in 1810, where he established a farm, began to use the name "Alday" and married a quarter-Seminole named "Red-Berry". This union is said to have produced two daughters, Samantha and one unnamed, and a number of sons, including James Daniel Alday, Sr., "Little-Berry", Benjamin, Redman or Redmond, Nathan, Fred, and others. From the advent of Little Berry Alday, records agree on the descent of Queen Esther Alday.

A third source, not necessarily independent, shows Little Berry Alday's father to have been Benjamin Ryan, born in 1772 in Burke County, Georgia, and his mother to have been Rhoda or RedBerry Berry, born in North Carolina in 1780. This source shows Little Berry's wife, Martha Faircloth, to have been the child of Matthew or Mather and Clarissa Sasser Faircloth, both born in 1803 in Screven County, Georgia.

Little Berry Alday, son of (possibly) Benjamin Alday, born either in Wilkinson County, Georgia 1816 or Baker County, Georgia in 1818, married Martha Faircloth (1825-1860), daughter of Mather and Clarissa Sasser Faircloth, and located, along with his brother Daniel, in Decatur, now Seminole County, Georgia. They had four children: Lucinda (1844- ?), Isaac Benjamin (1845/6-1881), Mathew (1846-1922), and Amanda (1860-1875/6), married to John R. Murkerson.

Isaac Benjamin Alday (some sources say Benjamin Isaac), son of Little Berry and Martha

Faircloth Alday, was born 9 February 1845 or 1846, in Baker County, Georgia. On 23 November 1865 he married Martha Johnson (24 December 1842 - 23 March 1927) in Decatur, now Seminole County, Georgia. Martha Johnson was the daughter of Jacob Johnson, Sr. (1808-1884) and Elizabeth Braswell (1812-1881). They had nine children: Jacob Sidney (1866-1883); Newton (1867-1877); Joseph (or Jasper) M. (1870-1894) who married Florence Plowden; Shandora Clarentine (1872-1933) who married Reverend Allen B. Ard; Martha Elizabeth (1873-?), who married Jesse G. Thompson; Littlebury H. (1875-1878); Isaac Benjamin, Jr. (1875-1878); Mary Lula (1877-?), who married Jim M. Sweat; and Queen Esther (1879-1936), who married John Eager Drake. (One record shows an additional daughter, Lula Lucinda, with no dates and married to Jim M. Sweat, shown above as husband of Mary Lula.)

Queen Esther Alday and John Eager Drake were married 13 July 1899 and had six surviving children...

Those children and their children, listed elsewhere in the work cited, were:

Ida Ethel Drake (1900-1995) married Ernest William Davis and had two children: Della Esther Davis (1921-2012) and William Middleton Davis II (1925-2016)

Claudia Rebecca Drake (1902-1986) married Lucius Tennille (1904-1971) and had two children: Charles Dean Tennille (1926-1970) and John Drake Tennille (1928-1987).

Johnie Mae Drake (1903-1996) married John Durward Kennedy (1906-2002) and had four children: Sarah Martha Kennedy (1929-   ), John Durward Kennedy, Jr. (1932-   ), Anna Susan Kennedy (1934-   ), Alan Russell Kennedy (1948-1998).

Herbert Eugene Drake (1905-1992), married Mamie Wells Bishop.

Lucille Drake (1906-1907).

Lillian Estelle Drake (1908-1999) married Clarence Floyd Bates (1908-2003) and had two children: Clarence Floyd Bates, Jr. (1932-1946) and John Walter Bates (1939-   ).

John Eager Drake, Jr. (1911-1967) married Willa Vesta Widener (   ) and had one child: Margaret Anne Drake (1935-).

Isaac
Benjamin
Alday

Martha
Johnson
Alday

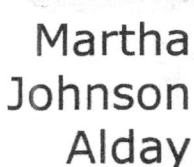

Alday Grave Markers

Isaac
Benjamin
Alday

1846 - 1881

Martha
Johnson
Alday

1842 - 1927

page from an Alday family Bible

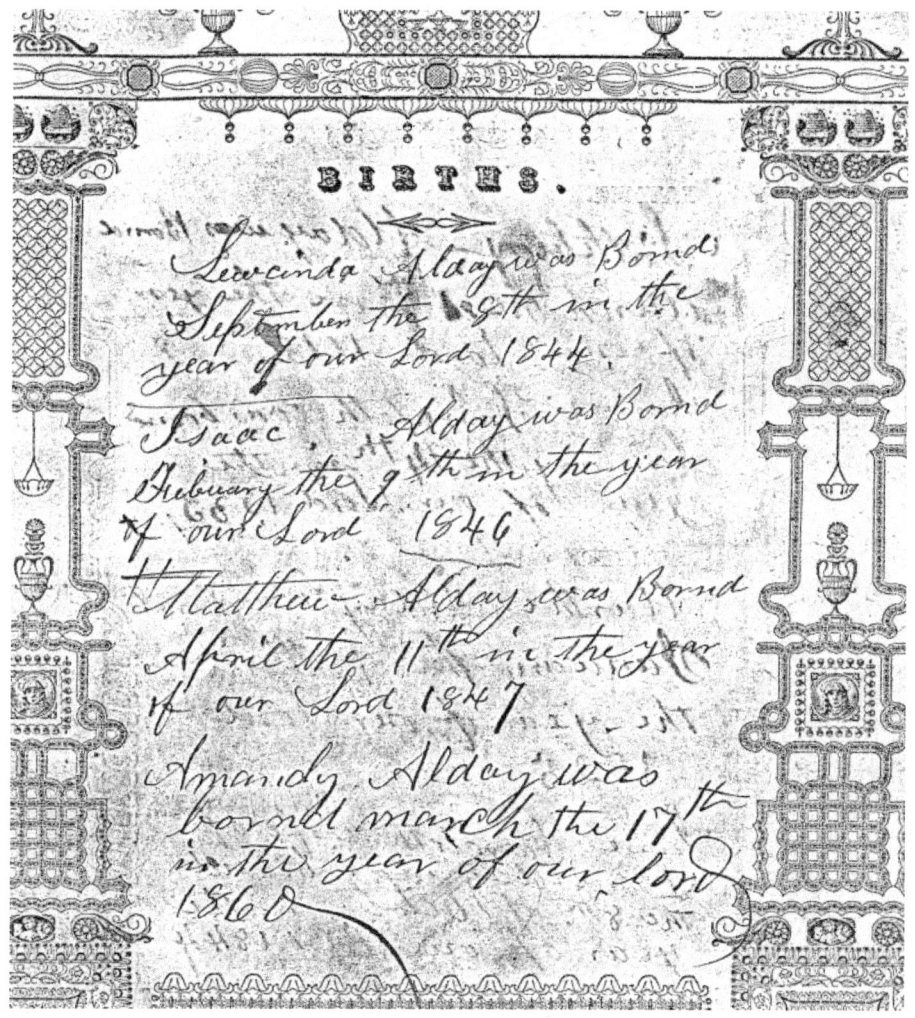

BIRTHS.

Lewcinda Alday was Bornd
September the 9th in the
year of our Lord 1844

Isaac Alday was Bornd
Febuary the 9th in the year
of our Lord 1846

Matthew Alday was Bornd
April the 11th in the year
of our Lord 1847

Amandy Alday was
bornd march the 17th
in the year of our Lord
1860

page from an Alday family Bible

MARRIAGES.

~~Green B Alday was Borned June the 4th in the year of our~~ Lord 1843

~~Green B Alday Deceast~~ December the 13th 1843

Littleberry Alday and Martha Faircloth was Married in Feby th last Day 1842

Littleberry Alday Mained Jane Faircloth Sept 1 1860

Asa C Alday Mairek Martha Johnson November the 16th 1865

page from an Alday family Bible

PARENTS' RECORD.

FATHER.

Littlebury Alday was Bornd March the 1th in the year of our Lord 1818 James Faircloth was borne January the 14th in the year of our Lord 1833

MOTHER.

Martha Alday was Bornd January the 16th in the year of our Lord 1825

Janey Faircloth wife of L.B Alday was bornd the 8th of October in the year of our lord 1844

page from an Alday family Bible

DEATHS.

Green B. Alday Deceast
December the 18th 1843

Rhody Alday Mother
of Littleberry Deceast the
11th of September 1851

Nancey an Elisabeth Thompson
Deceast this Life January
23d 1863

L. B. Alday Deceast
May the 10th 1868

Benjeman Thompson Deceast
this life November the first 1868
Mary Jane Roberts
Deceast this life october 31
1874

page from an Alday family Bible

1 Jacob ___ Alday was borend the 25th day of September in the year of our lord 1866

2 Newton Alday was borend the 24th day of March in the year of our lord 1868

3 Jasper Matthew Alday was born this 17th of May in the year of our lord 1870

No 4 J. D. C. F. ___ Alday born the 8th of October 187_

No 5 Martha Elizabeth Alday born the 22nd of ___ in the year ___ 18__

6 Isaac Baron Alday was born ___ our lord January the ___

Commentary on Cited Material

by John W. Bates

Perhaps the first genealogical exposition I ever saw up close was a six-page, typed piece entitled "This is the story of the origination of the names– Alday, Alda, Aulday, Alda, etc– Prepared, November 18, 1968 by Ralph Jackson Alday". It was handed to me with great elation by my aunt along with the words "See, we do have Indian blood!" In the middle years of the last century there were many who aspired to connect with the romance of the "noble savage" who was being treated very favorably at the time by movies and popular media. This was very different from earlier generations where the native American was considered by many Caucasians to be on an even lower social level than Negroes. This is the reason for my initial skepticism of the claims in the document. While possible, I think it unlikely that the children of a mixed marriage, especially those with close relatives continuing in mixed marriages as claimed by Mr. Alday, would become firmly established as substantial members of the predominantly white social class in Southwest Georgia during the latter part of the 19th and into the 20th Century. The Irish origin of the Alday name, corrupted from O'Day, seemed perfectly reasonable, and without countervailing evidence, acceptable. Mr. Alday's 1968 treatise, a copy of which is in the genealogical collection of the Seminole County Library in Donalsonville, Georgia is shown here.

This is the story of the origination of the names--

Alday, Alda, Aulday, Allda, etc--

Prepared, November 18, 1968 by: Ralph Jackson Alday
1202 East College Street
Bainbridge, Georgia 31717

Forward . . .

The first two generations of this story is not substatiated
except by heresay, passed on down to me, but this story, starting
with the third generation is very well proven out from such things
as civil war records (CSA), various census records of olden times,
tombstone markers, from different libraries that had books written
by various writers locally on local history, contacts with many living
relatives, tax records.

My family, my personal knowledge and in some cases from
family Bible, my mother has a remarkable memory for one who is
90 years old, some of my personal contacts of living relatives were
as old as 93 years of age.

Also, while reading this narrative, please keep in mind that in
the old days, most people were uneducated, or, at most, only partically
educated, and usually it was the duty of some members of each family
who was only partially educated to do the teaching of other members
of the family, or, of children only attending a makeshift part time
school for only a small portion of each year; particularly the
teaching and learning of spelling in old days was by sound of the
words. So you can readily see and understand how over the years that

One's name in the same family could consist of several various spellings within the same generation as well as in different generations.

To my own knowledge, even today, I have a lot of cousins who spell their surname about four different ways and I have heard of several other ways to spell "Alday", but this is the first and only history that I have heard of the origination of the surname of "Alday", "Allday", etc.

The different versions of spelling could very well be the results of legal papers, forms, marriage certificates, etc., in years long gone by, being filled out by a third party who could read and write after a fashion, such a city, county and state officials, doctors, lawyers, priests, ministers, bankers, politicians, large land owners, merchants, newspaper publishers, etc., some of these people having these forms and papers filled out could not even read or spell correctly, so the third person, in filling out these forms and legal papers would spell the person's name as it was pronounced, so in this way over the years, the same name could possibly have many different ways of spelling. In this story, the spelling of names is the as handed down to me. Also, I have met many "Aldays", "Allday", etc. in many other states who have traced their ancestors as far back as Georgia, and no further than the 1800's.

The following is the story of the origination of the surname –
Alday, Aldy, Alda, etc.

In the year of 1788 in Southeastern, Tennessee, near the
Georgia Border, a few miles east of Chattanooga, Tennessee, at the
edge of the Appalachian Mountains, an Irish imigrant known by
the name of "Red" or "Redman" (possibly Redmund) O'day, age 23,
given name not known unless it could have been "Redmund", married a
half breed Cherokee Indian maiden of about 15 years of age, whose
name was "Rain Deer", the only name she was ever known by.

It was said that Mr. O'Day's first name was not actually
recalled but that he was called "Red" of the color of his
hair and also called "Red-Man" possibly because he had married an
Indian girl.

Mr. O'day has been thought to have left a wife and two
children in some unknown part of Ireland when he came to America,
but after arriving here, he never saw or heard of them any more.

Out of this union of Mr. O'day and "Rain Deer" was born
one male child in the year of 1790, name Rain (later Rayn) O'day.
. . . later Alday, Allday, etc.; not other children were born of
this couple. It is said this Red O'day either died or was killed
in the year 1796, at the age of 31, near his home and was buried
there in SW Tennessee near the Georgia State line in an unmarked grave.

The child, Rayn O'Day was raised and cared for by his
mother and her people.

In the year of 1808, at the age of 18, Rain O'Day left his mother and his people in Tennessee and came to South West Georgia and settled in Baker County, Georgia as a farmer. No work was ever heard of the fate of his mother, Rain Deer.

Two years later in the year 1810 at the age of 20 Rayn O'Day married a quarter breed Seminole Indian maid of about 16 years of age, and henceforth Rain O'Day became known as "Rayn Alday". His quarter Indian wife was named "Red-Berry" was never known by any other name.

To this union were born a number of children, two girls and a number of boys, one of the girls was named Samantha, but the name of the other girl is unknown, one of the boys name was James Daniel Alday, Sr., born in 1817, and was my Great-Grandfather, Some of the names of the other boys were "Little-Berry" (El-Berry or L-Berry") born in 1816, Benjamin born in 1819, Redman (or Redmond) born in 1815; other boys - Nathan, Fred, R.F., Joseph, and Emanul. "Red-Berry" wife of Rayn Alday died about the same time as her husband, date unknown, both possibly could have been buried in the Indian mounds (Kolomoki) State Park - burial grounds near Beakley, Georgia in the northern part of Early County in South West Georgia. If this is not true, the burial place of both are unknown.

It is definitely known that some of these "off-springs" of this family married white people and some of them married people with part of Indian blook, mostly Creek and Seminole tribe, even some of the grand-children of Rayn Alday were definitely married to people of part Indian blood - a great number of the decendents of Rayn Alday family moved to the extreme Southwestern part of Georgia in southern Seminole County, South of Donalsonville, Georgia., the county when was Decatur County.

This moving took place during the years between years
from 1850 through 1858. Many of them died in that section of Georgia
and even today their decendents still live and flourish strongly in
that part of the state.

I have found the tombstone markers of both my great-grandparents
and grandparents graves in some cemetary in southern Seminole County
Georgia. At this date I am unable to find any of my relatives
still living in Baker County Georgia -- some of these desendents
are now known to be living in either parts of Georgia, also some
relatives live in Florida, Alabama, Mississippi, Louisiana, Tennessee,
Texas, California, and several other states, also I personally know
that many of the Aldays, male and female, are red headed.

It is also known that many of Ryan Alday's children and
grandchildren served with distinguished valar in various sections
of the confederate states of America (CSA). Armed Forces (Civil
War) with much personal sacrifice as so many other people did.
Some served as musicians in the infantry, calvary, heavy artillary
and most any other branch of the confederate army that you can
name. Also, it is known that many of Rayn Aldays desendents,
male and female, served faithfully in all wars from Civil up
to the present time. I definitely know that my great-grandfather
James Daniel Alday, Sr. and my grand-father, Green Benjamin Alday, Sr.
and many of their brothers served in the Civil War on the confederate
side, I might say here that in checking the exact birthdate of my
great-grandfather and my great father's family with the Civil War
records, I find that the actual birthdates do not agree. This was
due to the older one changing their birthdate to make them younger and
the younger to make them older in order to meet the requirements of
age for inlistments to the confederate army. I definitely know that
both my great-grandfather and grandfather served in the confederate

(GSA) and both changed their birthdays at the time to meet the

requirements for inlistments. I hope this story of mine will have

great interest for all who may read it, and in my personal analyzing

of this story, the mahor opinion of mine is that this story to me

seems very plausable. What is your opinion?

Countervailing evidence to Mr. Alday's story does appear in the published history of Seminole County, Georgia, also located in In the Seminole County, Georgia Library. In that history, The Alday family of Southwest Georgia is said to originate with Josiah Alday, of English descent, locating in Burke County, Georgia, by way of Virginia, in the 1760's.

Josiah's son, Benjamin, was the father of Littlebury Alday, the grandfather of Queen Esther. While there might be some confusion in the identification of "English" or "Irish" origin and the time when "O'Day" became "Alday" the time periods given are not compatible. If Josiah Alday located in the area which became Burke County, Georgia during the 1760's, then the family was located in the eastern coastal plain of Georgia for some years prior to the alleged appearance of O'Day from Ireland in the northwestern mountains.

Further contradiction of the Irish and native American legend comes from the DNA testing service of Ancestry.com. Analysis of my DNA reported in

November 2016 did show 16 percent Irish, but 60 percent Great Britain, 16 percent Western European and six percent divided between Northern Europe and Iberian Europe, for 98 percent. The remaining two percent is divided in fragments less than one percent each in the Middle East, the Caucasus and South Asia. No ethnic traces were reported for Africa, the Americas, Central, Northern or Eastern Asia, Eastern or Southern Europe or Pacific Islander. While the Irish ethnicity is present, the zero report for Native American should put the O'Day/Rain Deer legend to rest.

Queen Esther, like most people, left little physical memorial of her life. There may be some few today who have a brief childhood memory of her presence in their lives, but other than those memories the only information about her life is found in the documentation of statistical records, with one notable exception! Her husband, writing his memoir some ten or more years after her death did describe the moment when they first met and their marriage:

When I reached the age of eighteen years, a neighboring boy and myself decided to attend the closing of a singing school and the beginning of a revival meeting about thirteen miles from our home. We rode horse back for that distance, arriving at the church just as the service was beginning for the preaching hour. On entering the church, the congregation standing, we, with difficulty, found a place about midway the church of the left side of the aisle. There, we took our place. The music being made by the singers was very wonderful. After having taken my place in the church, I began to look over the congregation, that it, those in front and to my left and right, not looking backward of course. I looked down at the church organ and there I beheld a very beautiful, young girl performing on the instrument and singling alto at the same time. Her appearance naturally attracted my undivided attention during the entire services of the day. Just before the service was over, I had an opportunity to speak to a young man on my right side and asked him who the young lady at the organ was. He gave me her name and stated, "When services are over, if you would like to meet her, I will take you up and introduce you". I assured him it would be my pleasure. After the benediction was said, we made our way up to the front of the pulpit, where she and some other young ladies were standing. Of course, they observed us approaching them. She turned around. He spoke to her and gave the proper introduction. I began an immediate conversation with her and asked for permission to escort her home, to which request she consented. This was the beginning of a romance which ended some three and a half years later by this young lady having become my wife.[7]

. . .

In the latter part of 1899, the subject of this story was married to the young lady whom he had discovered some three years prior performing at the church organ at a country church. To this union were born five daughters and two sons, one of the daughters having died in infancy at the age of four months.[8]

In relating his first sight of Queen Esther, John

---

[6] The Seventh Child (pp 72-73)
[7] Ibid, p101

comments on her playing the organ and singing. She apparently had significant natural musical talent which was passed on to all of her daughters to some extent but especially to her daughter Johnie who provided music for groups and organizations for much of her adult life. Daughter Lillian claimed that her mother could pick up any instrument and without coaching achieve at least a basic level of performance skill in a short time.

Typical of her time, Queen Esther was a home body, cooking, cleaning, attending to the children and to her husband while on the farm, after moving into Iron City proper and then after relocating to Bainbridge. As most rural and semi-rural families with property, she surely had house servants and, from stories shared, she used much of her time playing with children and grandchildren. Grandson William Davis shared a photograph of her in the front yard of the Bainbridge house at 319 South West Street (later redesignated 721). This picture from around 1930 shows Queen Esther, daughter Ida Davis and grandchildren Della Esther Davis and William Davis resting.

Probably from an earlier time, the next picture is of members of the family and   others not identified enjoying the waters of the Gulf of Mexico at Panacea,

Florida.   The group appears to include Ida, John Eager, Jr. and Queen Esther in the center of activity. She seemed to enjoy her children and, from all reports, her children enjoyed her. A member of her children's generation who was a neighbor on South West Street once remarked that she spent far too much time in the yard playing with the children. The remark may have been meant negatively in the context of the previous century, but resounds to Queen Esther's credit today.

Findings from Analysis of Ancestry.Com Family Tree Data and Tracking Antecedents of Queen Esther Alday[9] Along a Single Line to 1028 CE

Queen Esther Alday was born 15 October 1879 in Cuthbert, Randolph County, Georgia, the daughter of Benjamin Isaac Alday (1846-1881) and Martha Johnson Alday (1842-1927). She married John Eager Howard Drake (1879-1964) on 13 July 1899 in Decatur County, Georgia. They had seven children: Ida Ethel (1900-1995) who married Ernest William Davis; Claudia Rebecca (1902-1986), who married Lucius Tennille; Johnie Mae (1903-1996), who married John Durward Kennedy; Herbert Eugene (1905-1992), who married Mamie Bishop Wells; Lillian Estelle (1909-1999), who married Clarence Floyd Bates; and John Eager, Jr. (1911-1967), who married Willavesta Widner. Queen Esther died March 13, 1936 in Bainbridge, Decatur County, Georgia.

Benjamin Isaac Alday was born 9 February 1846 in Baker County, Georgia, the son of Littlebury L. B. Alday (1816-1866) and Martha Faircloth (1825-1860). He married Martha Johnson, probably in 1865. They had at least eight children: Jacob Sydney (1866-1883); Newton (1870-1894) who married Florence Plowden; Shandora Clarentine (1872-1933) who married Allen. B. Ard; Martha Elizabeth (1873- ?) who married Jesse G. Thompson;

---

[6] Various sources and various generations show spelling of both "Alday" and Allday. For consistency the "Alday" spelling will be used throughout this narrative.

Littlebury H. (1875-1828); Isaac Benjamin, Jr. (1875-1878); Mary Lula[10] (1877- ?) who married Jim M. Sweat; and **Queen Esther (1879-1936)** who married John Eager Howard Drake. He died 20 February 1881 in Decatur County (now Seminole), Georgia.

Littlebury L. B. Alday was born in 1816 in Baker County, Georgia, the son of Benjamin Ryan Alday (1772-1840) and Rhoda Redberry Berry (1794-1839). He married Martha Faircloth (1825-1860) in 1843. They had three children: **Benjamin Isaac (1846-1881)** who married Martha Johnson (1842-1927); Matthew Alday (1847-1922); and Amanda Alday (1860-1920). Littleberry Alday married Jane Faircloth (1843-1924) in 1860. He died in 1866 in Decatur County, Georgia.

Benjamin Ryan Alday was born in 1772 in Burke County, Georgia, the son of Josiah Alday (1747-1820) and Anne Womack (1745-1772). He married Rhoda Redberry Berry (1794-1839). They had six children: James Alday (1810- ?); John Benjamin Alday (1811-1840); Benjamin Isaac Alday (1811-1840); Mary Ann Alday (1813-1860); Redman Wilbur Alday (1815-1893) and **Littleberry L. B. Alday (1816-1866)** who married Martha Faircloth and subsequently Janet Faircloth. He died in 1840 in Early County, Georgia.

---

[7]one record shows an additional daughter with no dates given and who is shown to have married Jim M. Sweat, the name reported elsewhere for the husband of Mary Lula.

Josiah Alday was born in 1747 in Ludenburg, Virginia, the son of Perrin Alday 1700 - ?) and Francis Hannah Lockett (1721-1805). He married Anne Womack (1745-1772). They had one son, **Benjamin Ryan Alday (1722-1840)** who married Rhoda Redberry Berry (1794-1839). He died in 1820 in Wilkinson or Burke County, Georgia.

> *Two marriages are listed for Josiah Alday: Frances Hannah Locket (1721-1805) and Susannah Allen (1730-1803). There is a record of the marriage to Susannah Allen in Goochland, Virginia on 7 October 1785 but as yet none found for the marriage to Frances Hannah. Josiah is shown to have been born in 1747, well prior to the date given for Josiah's marriage to Susannah and when Frances Hannah would have been about 26 years old and Susannah 17. My surmise is that the date for Frances's death is in error and should be 1785 or sooner. This discrepancy is not of concern in this narrative since the line of descent is on the father's side so precision of designation of maternity is not significant.*

Perrin Alday was born in 1700 in Henrico County, Virginia, the son of John Alday (1660-1710) and Elizabeth Perrin (1675-1748). He married Frances Hannah Locket (1721-1805). They had one son, **Josiah Alday (1747-1820)** who married Anne Womack (1745-1772). He was also married to Susannah Allen (1730-1803). He died in Charlotte, Virginia reportedly at the age of 105 on July 30, 1805.

> *While living to the age of 105 is not impossible, at the time it is somewhat improbable. Note that the 1805 year of death given for Perrin is the same (possibly incorrect) year of death for his daughter-in-law Frances Hannah Locket.*

John Alday was born in 1660 in Westmoreland, Virginia, the son of Henry Alday (1630-1670) and Grace Gray (1643-1670). He married Elizabeth Perrin (1675-1748) in 1707 and they had six children: John Alday (1695-), Sarah Alday (1698-); **Perrin**

Alday (1700-1805), who married Francis Hannah Lockett and Susannah Allen; Thomas Allday (1705-1754); Seth Alday (?); and Benjamin Alday (?). He died in 1710 in Henrico, Virginia.

> *While Henry Alday is shown to have had two sons with the name "John", the one noted here and another born in Henrico, Virginia in 1670 and living until 1750. No other information, particularly identification of spouse and/or children is known from available sources. It may be possible that this is a duplicate entry for the same person but with different years of birth and death. Again, however, the possible discrepancy is not relevant since the ancestral line here is being traced through the father Henry Alday, who is clearly the father of either of these two John Aldays.*

Henry Alday was born in 1630 in London, England, the son of Samuel Alday (1600-1650) and Sarah Elizabeth Jones (1601-1650). He immigrated to Virginia and married Grace Gray (1643-1670) on June 5, 1661. They had four children: **John Alday (1660-1710)** who married Elizabeth Perrin; Ann Alday (1663-); Mary Alday (1665-1710); and John Alday (1670-1750) [*see note above concerning possible duplication of entries*]. He died April 27, 1670 in Westmoreland, Virginia.

Sarah Elizabeth Jones was born in London, England in 1601, the daughter of William Jones (1563-1633) and Elizabeth (Bodenham) Morgan (1572-1650). She married Samuel Allday (1565[?]-1650). They had one son, **Henry Alday (1630-1670)** who immigrated to Virginia and married Grace Gray. Samuel Alday died around 1650 in London. Sarah also died in London in 1650.

> *At this point the Queen Esther Alday ancestral line reported here will depart from the Alday line and turn to the ancestors of Samuel Alday's wife, Sarah Elizabeth Jones.*

William Jones was born in Abergravenny, Monmouth England in 1563, the son of Sir Henry (Berekely) Jones (1534-1574) and Catherine Morgan Machen Tredegar (1544-1574). He married Elizabeth (Bodenham) Morgan and they had one daughter, **Sarah Elizabeth Jones (1601-1650)** who married Samuel Alday (1600-1650). He died in Northhamptonshire, England in 1633.

Catherine Morgan Machen Tredegar was born in 1544 in Tredegar, Monmouthshire, Wales, the youngest child of Morgan, Baron Morgan, Sir Rowland of Machen and Tredegar (1508-1577) and Lady Blanch Thomas, Baroness Morgan (1512-1579). In 1562 she married Sir Henry [Berkely] Jones (1534-1574). They had four children: John Jones (1555-?); **William (1563-1633)** who married Elizabeth (Bodenham) Morgan; Thomas (1565-?) and Sarah (?). Catherine died in Monmouthshire, Wales in 1574.

At this point the Queen Esther Alday ancestral line reported here will depart from the Jones line and turn to the ancestors of William Jones' wife, Catherine Morgan.

Morgan, Baron Morgan, Sir Rowland of Machen and Tredegar was born in 1508 in Machen, Gwynilwg, Monmouthshire, Wales, the son of Thomas Mather Machen Tredegar Morgan (1482-1538) and Elizabeth Talgarth Vaughan (1486-1528). He married Lady Blanch Thomas, Baroness Morgan (1512-1579) in 1530 in Monmouthshire, Wales. They had ten children: Thomas (1520-1577); William (1532-1629); Ann Morgan Machen Tredegar (1533-1538); Thomas Morgan (1534-1603); Amy Morgan (1535-1538); Henry Morgan (1536-1603);

Mary Morgan (1536-1536); Sir Henry Morgan [Governor of Jamaica?] (1536-1567); Elizabeth Morgan (1538-1538); and **Catherine Morgan Machen Tredegar (1544-1574)** who married Sir Henry [Berkely] Jones. He died in Machen, Gwynilwg, Monmouthshire, Wales in 1577.

Thomas Mather Machen Tredegar Morgan was born in Thredegar, Nmnth, Wales in 1482, the son of Roger Morgan (1436-1500) and Lady Jane, Baroness Vaughan Whitney (1460-1550). He married Elizabeth Talgarth Vaugh (1486-1528) in 1498. They had one son, **Morgan, Baron Morgan, Sir Rowland of Machen and Tredegar (1508-1577)**. He died in 1538 in Llangurig, Montgomeryshire, Wales.

> *At this point the Queen Esther Alday ancestral line reported here will depart from the Morgan line and pass through three generations of maternal descent.*

Lady Jane, Baroness Vaughan Whitney was born in 1460 at Whitney Hall, Herefordshire, England, the daughter of Sir Robert Whitney Whitney KB (1436–1480) and Constance Lady Staffordshire Touchet (1443-1531). She married Roger Morgan (1436-1500) in 1485 and they had one son, **Thomas Mather Machen Tredegar Morgan (1482-1538)** who married Elizabeth Talgarth Vaugh (1486-1528). Lady Jane died in 1550 in Talgarth, Breconshire, Wales.

Constance Touchet, Lady Staffordshire , was born in April 1443 at Heleigh Castle, Staffordshire, England, the daughter of Sir James Touchet (Tuchet) , 5th Lord Audley (1398–1459) and Eleanor de Holland (1405–1459). In 1448 she married Sir Robert

Whitney. Lord Whitney KB (1436–1480) at Whitney Hall, Herefordshire, England. They had five children: **Lady Jane, Baroness Vaughan Whitney (1460-1550)** who married Roger Morgan; Sir James Whitney, Lord Whitney (1465-1541); John Whitney (1471-1471); Robert Whitney (1474-1495); and James Whitney (1544-1587). She died in 1531 in Hereford, Herefordshire, England.

Eleanor de Holland was born 5 October 1405 in Kenilworth, Warwickshire England, the daughter of Edmond Holland (1384-1408) and Constance Plantagenet (1374-1416). She married Sir James Touchette, Lord Audley on 14 February 1429 and they had a daughter **Constance (1443-1531)** who married Sir Robert Whitney, Lord Whitney KB (1436–1480). She died 23 September 1459 at Heleigh Castle, Staffordshire.

> *Eleanor de Holland's father and mother shared a thrice-great grandfather, descended from different wives. In addition, her paternal grandmother was descended from a brother of that common ancestor. This narrative will proceed in parallel from Eleanor's father, first through his maternal line to the brother and then through the paternal line to her parents' (first) shared ancestor. The narrative will then proceed on her maternal line of descent.*

Edmund Holland Earl of Kent was born 6 January 1384, the second son of Thomas Holland (1350-1397) and Alice Fitzalan (1350-1416). He succeeded to the Earldom on the death of his childless brother Thomas (1374-1400) and was married to Lucia Visconti (1370-1424) but had no children from this marriage. He had a daughter, **Eleanor de Holland (1405-1459)** from a liaison with Constance Plantagenet (1374-1416). Edmund was killed in the Battle of Ile-de-Brehat on 15 September 1408 and was buried on the Island of Lavrec in the Brehat Archipelago.

Edmund Holland's mother, Alice Fitzalan, was a direct descendent of Henry III Plantagenet through his younger son Edmund [Crouchback].

Alice Fitzalan[11] was born in 1350 in Arundel Castle in Sussex England, the daughter of Richard Fitzalan, Duke of Arundel (1306/13-1376) and his second wife, Eleanor [Plantagenet] of Lancaster (1318-1372). On 10 April 1364 she married Thomas Holland (1350/54-1397) and they had three sons and six daughters: Eleanor [Alainore] (1373-1405); Thomas (1374-1400); Joan (1380-1434); John (?); **Edmund (1384-1408)**; Margaret (1385-1439); Eleanor II [Alainore] (1386-1413); Elizabeth (1387-1420); and Bridget (?). Alice died 17 March 1416, possibly in Middlesex and may be buried in Westminster.

Eleanor [Plantagenet] of Lancaster was born 11 September 1318 at Grosmont Castle, Grosmont, Monnouthshire, the daughter of Henry Plantagenet, 3rd Earl of Lancaster (1281-1345) and Maud Chaworth (1282-1322). On 6 November 1330 Eleanor married John de Beaumont (1318-1342) and they had one child. On 5 February 1344 at Ditton Church, Stoke Poges, Buckinghamshire, Eleanor married Richard Fitzalan (1306/13-1376) and they had seven children: Richard (1346-1397); John (1349-1379)l Thomas Arundel (1353-1413); Joan

---

[7] The name is shown in various sources as "Fitzalan", "FitzAlan" and "Fitz Alan". For consistency "Fitzalan" will be used here.

(1347-1419); **Alice (1350-1416)** who married Thomas Holland (1350-1397); Mary (?-1396); and Eleanor (1356-1366). Eleanor died 11 January 1372 and was buried in Lewes Priory, Sussex.

Henry Plantagenet, 3rd Earl of Lancaster was born in 1281 at Grosmont Castle, Monmouthshire, the son of Edmund [Crouchback] [12] Plantagenet (1245-1296) and Blanche of Artois (1248-1302). Sometime before 2 March 1297 he married Maud [Matilda] de Chaworth (1282-1322) and they had seven children: Blanche (1302/5-1380); Henry (1310-1361); Maud (1310-1377); Joan (1312-1345); Isabel (1318-1372); **Eleanor (1318-1372)** who married John de Beaumont (1318-1342) and Richard Fitzalan (1306/13-1376); and Mary (1320-1362). Henry died 22 September 1345 in Leicester Monastery of Cannons, Leicester, Leicestershire and was buried in Newark Abbey in Leicester.

Edmund [Crouchback] Plantagenet was born 16 January 1245 in London, the younger son of Henry III, Plantagenet (1207-1272) and Eleanor of Provence (1223-1291). On 8 April 1269 he married Aveline de Forze (1259-1274) in Westminster Abbey. They had no children. Between 28 July and 29 October 1276, in Paris, Edmund married Blanche of Artois (1248-1302) who was the widow of King Henry of Navarre and regent for her daughter Queen Joan who was betrothed to Prince Philip [Philip IV]. Edmund and Blanche had three sons: Thomas

---

[8] "Crouchback" or "crossed back" may be a refrence to Edmund wearing the emblem of a cross on his back to show his participation in the ninth crusade.

(1278-1322) **Henry (1281-1345)** who married Maud [Matilda] de Chaworth (1282-1322); and John (1286-1317). There may also have been a daughter Mary. Edmund died on 5 June 1296 in Bayonne, Duchy of Acquitaine, and was buried in Westminister Abbey.

Edmund Holland's father, Thomas Holland, was a direct descendent of Edward I Plantagenet through his second wife, Margaret of France.

Thomas Holland [de Holand] was born in 1350 (or 1354) in Upholand, Lancashire England, the son of Thomas Holland (1314-1360) and Joan Plantagenet [The Fair Maid of Kent] (1328-1385). On 10 April 1364 he married Alice Fitzalan (1350-1416) and they had three sons and six daughters: Eleanor [Alainore] (1373-1405); Thomas (1374-1400); Joan (1380-1434); John (?); **Edmund (1384-1408)**; Margaret (1385-1439); Eleanor II [Alainore] (1386-1413); Elizabeth (1387-1420); and Bridget (?). Thomas died 25 April 1397 at Arundel Castle, Sussex and was buried at Bourne Abbey in Lincolnshire.

Joan Plantagenet was born 29 September 1328 at Woodstock Palace, Oxfordshire (Wallingford, Berkshire), the daughter of Edmund of Woodstock (1301-1330) and Margaret Wake (1297-1349). In 1340 she married, in secret, Thomas Holland (1314-1360) prior to his departure for foreign wars. While he was away she was forced to marry the Earl of Salisbury, but upon Holland's return he claimed his wife and the Salisbury marriage was annulled. Joan and Thomas had five children: **Thomas (1350/54-1399)**; John (1352-1400); Joan

(1356-1384); Maud (1359-1391); and Edmund (1354-1354). After the death of Thomas in 1360 Joan married Edward Plantagenet [The Black Prince] (1330-1376) and they had two sons: Edward (1365-1370) and Richard (1367-1400) who succeeded his grandfather Edward III as Richard II. Joan died 7 August 1385 at Woodstock Palace and was buried in Stamford, Lincolnshire.

Edmund of Woodstock, 1st Earl of Kent, was born 5 August 1301 at Woodstock in Oxfordshire, the second son of Edward I, Plantagenet (1239-1307) and Edward's second wife Margaret of France (1279-1318). He married Margaret Wake in December 1325 and they had four children: Edmund (1326-1331); Margaret (1327-1352); **Joan (1328-1385)** who married Thomas Holland (1314-1360) and John (1330-1352). Edmund was executed 19 March 1330 at Winchester Castle during the regency of his half-nephew Edward III, whom upon coming of age and assuming full powers annulled the charge of treason and returned the Kent Estates to Edmund's son and Edmund was buried in Westminister Abbey.

Eleanor de Holland's mother, Constance of York, was a direct descendant of Henry III, Plantagenet, through his son Edward and Edward's first wife Eleanor of Castile.

Constance of York was born in 1374 at Conisburgh Castle in Yorkshire, the only daughter of Edmund [Langley] Plantagenet and Isabella of Castile (1355-1392). She married Thomas le Dispenser (1373-1400) on 7 November 1379, and they had two children surviving infancy: Richard (1396-1414); and Isabel (1400-1439). After the death of her husband in 1400 she was in a relationship with Edmund Holland which yielded a daughter **Eleanor de Holland (1405-1459)**. Constance died 24 November 1416 in Reading Abbey, Berkshire England where she was buried.

Edmund [Langley] Plantagenet, 1st Duke of York, was born 5 June 1341 in Kings Langley Palace in Herefordshire England, the fourth surviving son of Edward III, Plantagenet (1312-1377) and Philippa of Hainaut (1314-1369). On 11 July 1372 he married Isabella of Castile (1355-1392) at Wallingford, Oxfordshire. They had three children: Edward Langley (1373-1415), **Constance (1374-1416)** who married Thomas le Despenser and later had a child with **Edmund Holland (1382-1408)**; and Richard (1375-1415). Edmund died 1 August 1402 at Kings Langley Palace where he was buried.

Edward III, Plantagenet, King of England, was born 13 November 1312 at Windsor, Berkshire England, the eldest son of Edward II, Plantagenet (1284-1327) and Isabella (Capet) of France (1295-1358). On 24 January 1328 he formally married Philippa of Hainaut (1314-1369) in York Minster. They had a number of children including: Edward (1330-1376); Isabella (1332-1382); Joan (1334-1348); William [Hatfield] (1337-1337); Lionel (1338-1368);John (1340-1399); **Edmund (1341-1402)** who married Isabella of Castile (1355-1392); Blanche (1342-1342); Mary (1344-1362); Margaret (1346-1361); Thomas [Windsor] (1347-1348); William [Windsor] (1348-1348); and Thomas [Woodstock] (1355-1397). Edward died 21 June 1377 at Sheen,

Richmond, and was buried in Westminster Abbey.

Edward II, Plantagenet, King of England was born 25 April 1284 in Caernarfon Castle, Gwynedd, North Wales, the fourth and only surviving son of Edward I, Plantagenet (1239-1307) and his first wife, Eleanor of Provence (1223-1249). On 25 January 1308 he married, in Boulogne, Isabella (Capet) of France (1295-1358), the daughter of Philip IV. They had four children: **Edward (1312-1377)** who married Philippa of Hainaut (1314-1369); John (1316-1336); Eleanor (1318-1355); and Joan (1321-1355). Edward died 21 September 1327 in Gloucestershire, England and was buried in Gloucester Cathedral.

Edward I, Plantagenet, King of England was born 18 June 1239 in the Palace of Westminister, the eldest son of Henry III (1207-1272) and Eleanor of Provence (1223-1246). In 1254 he married Eleanor of Castile (1241-1290) and they had a number of children, several of whom did not survive infancy and childhood. Among the surviving children were: Eleanor (1269-1298); Joan (1272-1307); Alphonso(127-1284); Margaret (1275-1333); Mary (1279-1332); Elizabeth (1282-1316); and **Edward (1284-1327)** who married Isabella of France (1295-1358). In 1299 Edward married Margaret of France (1279-1318) and they had three children: Thomas (1300-1338); **Edmund (1301-1330)**; and Eleanor (1306-1311). Edward died 7 July 1307 at Burgh by Sands, Cumberland England and was buried in Westminister Abbey.

Henry III, Plantagenet, King of England was born 1 October 1207 in Winchester Castle, the eldest son of

John I (1166-1216) and Isabella of Angoloume (1188-1246). In 1236 he married Eleanor Berrengier [of Provence] (1223-1291) and they had five children: **Edward (1239-1307)** who married Eleanor of Castile (1241-1290) and Margaret of France (1279-1318); Margaret (1240-1275); Beatrice (1242-1275); **Edmund (1245-1296)** who married Aveline Forze (1259-1274) without issue and Blanche of Artois (1248-1302); and Katherine (1253-1257). Henry died 16 November 1272 in Westminster and was buried in Westminster Abbey.

John I, Plantagenet, King on England was born 24 December 1166 at Beaumont Palace, Oxford England, the youngest son of Henry II (1133-1189) and Eleanor of Acquitaine (1122-1204). In 1189 he married Isabella, Countess of Glouster (1173-1217) but that marriage was annulled in 1199. They had no children. In 1200 John married Isabella of Angouleme (1188-1246) and they had five children: **Henry (1216-1272)** who married Eleanor of Provence (1223-1291); Richard (1209-1272); Joan (1210-1238); Isabella (1214-1241); and Eleanor (1215-1275). John died during the night of 18/19 October 1216 in Newark Castle, Nottinghamshire and was buried in Worcester Cathedral.

Henry II, Plantagenet, King of England was born 5 March 1133 in Le Mans, France, the son of Geoffrey of Anjou (1113-1155) and Matilda Beauclerc (1102-1167). He married Eleanor, Duchess of Acquitaine (1122-1204), in 1152. They had eight children: William (1153-1156); Henry (1155-1183); Matilda (1156-1189); Richard (1157-1199); Geoffrey (1158-1186); Eleanor (1161-1214); Joan

(1165-1199); and **John (1166-1216)** who married Isabella of Angouleme (1888-1246). Henry died 6 July 1189 at Chinon Castle in France and was buried at the Fontevraud Abbey.

Matilda Beauclerc (Empress Maud, Queen Maud) was born 7 November 1102 in Sutton Courteney, Oxfordshire, England, the daughter of Henry I, King of England (1028-1087) and Matilda of Scotland (1080-1118). She was married in January 1114 to Henry IV, Salian, King of Germany, King of Rome and Holy Roman Emperor (1081-1125), but had no children in that marriage. After the death of Henry V she returned from Germany to Normandy and on 17 June 1128 she married Geoffrey Plantagenet[13] (1113-1151), son of Foulques V, Count of Anjou. They had three sons: **Henry Plantagenet (1133-1189)** who married Eleanor of Acquitaine (1122-1204); Geoffrey VI, Count of Nantes (1134-1158); and William FitzEmpress (1136-1164). Matilda died on 10 September 1167 in Normandy and was buried in the abbey of Bec-Hellouin.

Henry I (Beauclerc), King of England, was born around 1068, the fourth son of William of Normandy (1028-1087) and Matilda of Flanders (1031-1083). Left landless by his father, he seized the crown of England on the death of his brother William Rufus (1056-1100). He married Matilda of Scotland (1080-1118), daughter of Malcom III, and they had

---

[9] Geoffrey was called "Plantagenet" after his practice of wearing a yellow sprig of broom blossom (planta genista). His domain of Anjou was also the source of the epiphet "Angevin" applied to his descendents' rule and domains.

two children: **Matilda Beauclerc**[5] **(1102-1167)**, who married Geoffrey Plantagent (1113-1150), and William Adelin (1103-1120). There may have been another son, Richard, who died young if he existed. In 1121 Henry married Adeliza of Louvain (1103-1151). This marriage was childless. Henry died 1 December 1135 in the area of Lyons-la-Foret in France. His body was buried at Reading Abbey in England.

William I, King of England (William the Conqueror, William of Normandy, William the Bastard) was born around 1028 in Falaise Normandy (France), the illegitimate son of Robert I, Duke of Normandy (?-1035) and a concubine Herleva (Arlette). In 1049 he married Matilda, daughter of Baldwin V, Count of Flanders (1031-1083) and they had nine known children: Robert, Duke of Normandy (1051-1134); Richard (1054-1075); William Rufus (1056-1100); **Henry Beauclerc (1068-1135)**, who married Matilda of Scotland (1080-1118); Agatha; Adeliza (Adelida, Adelaide); Cecilia (Cecily); Matilda; Constance; and Adela. William died on 9 September 1987 in Rouen and was buried in Caen.

Summary Tabulation of Ancestry of Queen Esther Alday

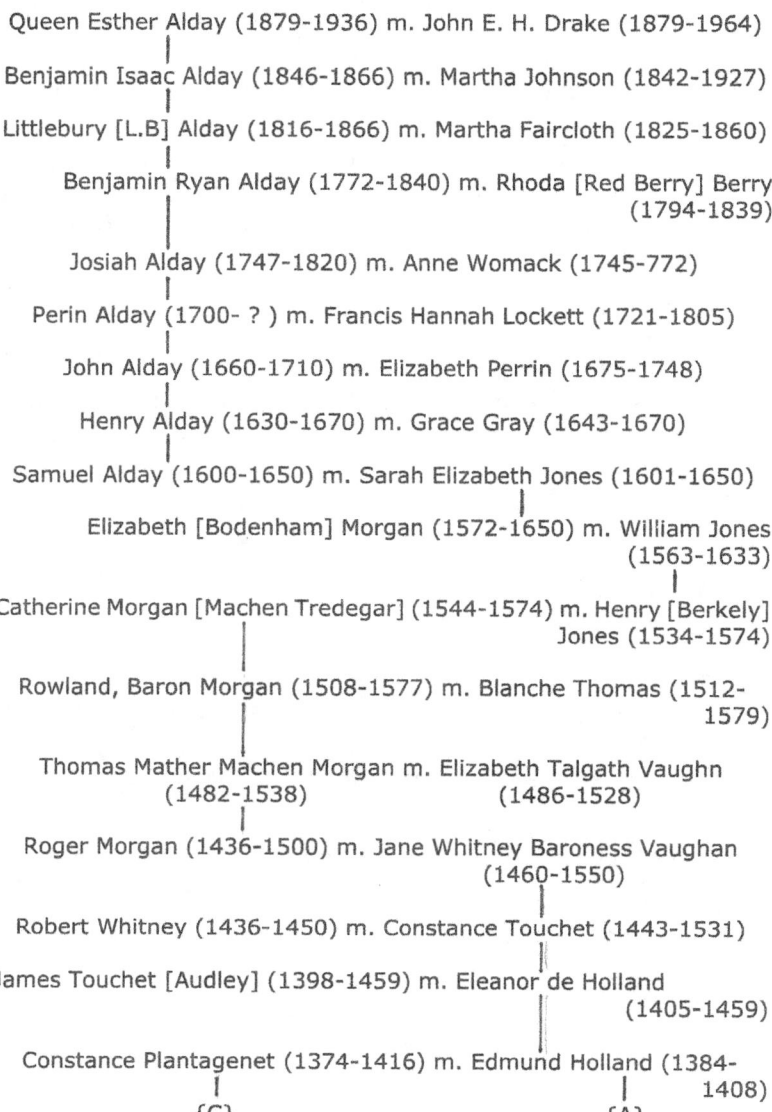

Queen Esther Alday (1879-1936) m. John E. H. Drake (1879-1964)

Benjamin Isaac Alday (1846-1866) m. Martha Johnson (1842-1927)

Littlebury [L.B] Alday (1816-1866) m. Martha Faircloth (1825-1860)

Benjamin Ryan Alday (1772-1840) m. Rhoda [Red Berry] Berry (1794-1839)

Josiah Alday (1747-1820) m. Anne Womack (1745-772)

Perin Alday (1700- ?) m. Francis Hannah Lockett (1721-1805)

John Alday (1660-1710) m. Elizabeth Perrin (1675-1748)

Henry Alday (1630-1670) m. Grace Gray (1643-1670)

Samuel Alday (1600-1650) m. Sarah Elizabeth Jones (1601-1650)

Elizabeth [Bodenham] Morgan (1572-1650) m. William Jones (1563-1633)

Catherine Morgan [Machen Tredegar] (1544-1574) m. Henry [Berkely] Jones (1534-1574)

Rowland, Baron Morgan (1508-1577) m. Blanche Thomas (1512-1579)

Thomas Mather Machen Morgan m. Elizabeth Talgath Vaughn
(1482-1538)   (1486-1528)

Roger Morgan (1436-1500) m. Jane Whitney Baroness Vaughan (1460-1550)

Robert Whitney (1436-1450) m. Constance Touchet (1443-1531)

James Touchet [Audley] (1398-1459) m. Eleanor de Holland (1405-1459)

Constance Plantagenet (1374-1416) m. Edmund Holland (1384-1408)

{C}   {A}

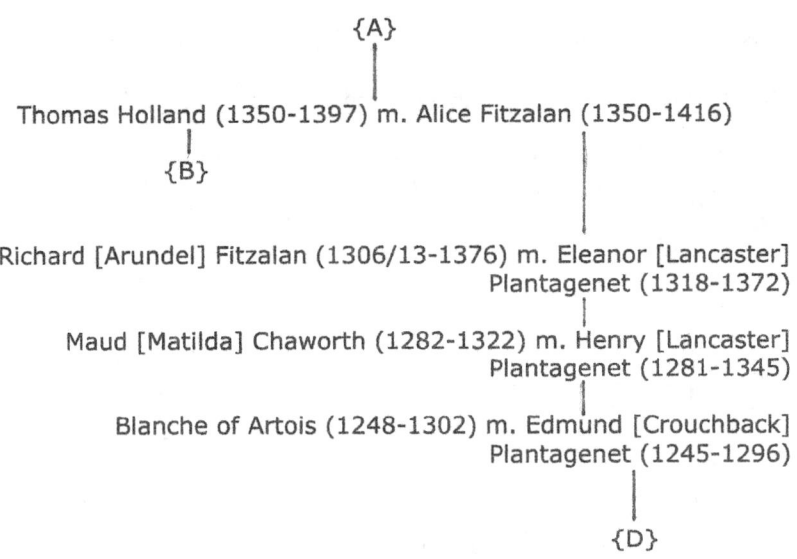

{A}

Thomas Holland (1350-1397) m. Alice Fitzalan (1350-1416)

{B}

Richard [Arundel] Fitzalan (1306/13-1376) m. Eleanor [Lancaster]
Plantagenet (1318-1372)

Maud [Matilda] Chaworth (1282-1322) m. Henry [Lancaster]
Plantagenet (1281-1345)

Blanche of Artois (1248-1302) m. Edmund [Crouchback]
Plantagenet (1245-1296)

{D}

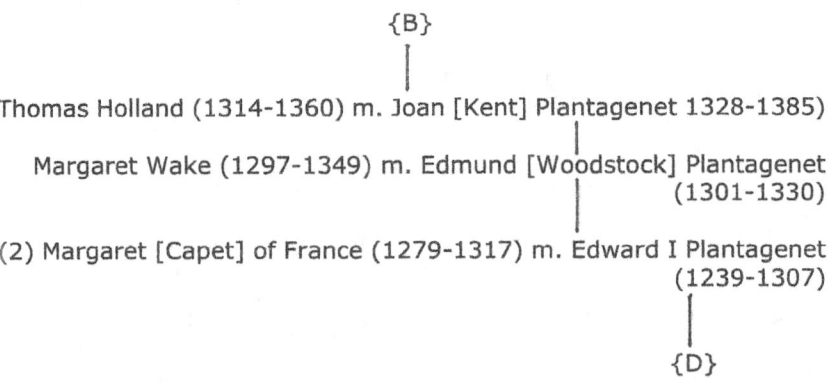

{B}

Thomas Holland (1314-1360) m. Joan [Kent] Plantagenet 1328-1385)

Margaret Wake (1297-1349) m. Edmund [Woodstock] Plantagenet
(1301-1330)

(2) Margaret [Capet] of France (1279-1317) m. Edward I Plantagenet
(1239-1307)

{D}

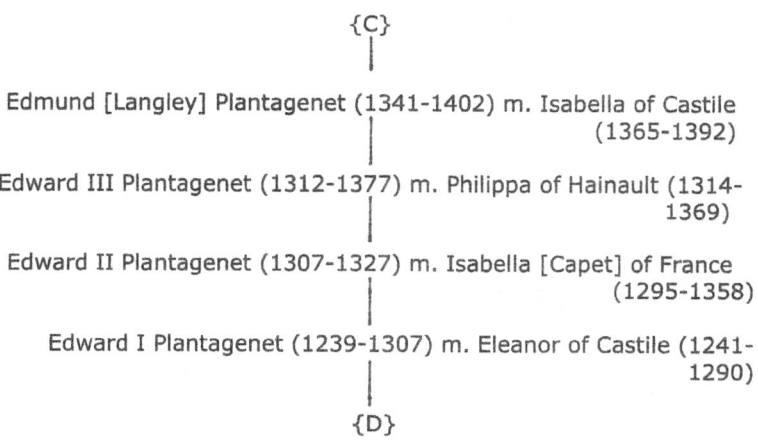

{C}

Edmund [Langley] Plantagenet (1341-1402) m. Isabella of Castile (1365-1392)

Edward III Plantagenet (1312-1377) m. Philippa of Hainault (1314-1369)

Edward II Plantagenet (1307-1327) m. Isabella [Capet] of France (1295-1358)

Edward I Plantagenet (1239-1307) m. Eleanor of Castile (1241-1290)

{D}

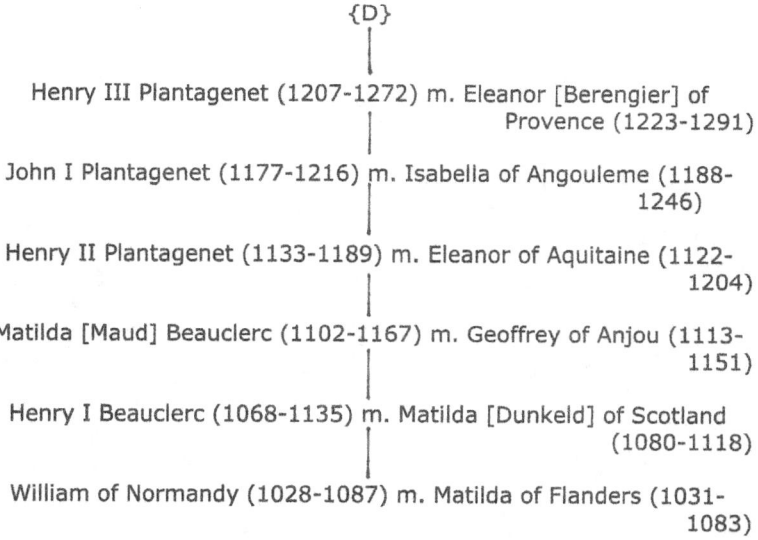

{D}

Henry III Plantagenet (1207-1272) m. Eleanor [Berengier] of Provence (1223-1291)

John I Plantagenet (1177-1216) m. Isabella of Angouleme (1188-1246)

Henry II Plantagenet (1133-1189) m. Eleanor of Aquitaine (1122-1204)

Matilda [Maud] Beauclerc (1102-1167) m. Geoffrey of Anjou (1113-1151)

Henry I Beauclerc (1068-1135) m. Matilda [Dunkeld] of Scotland (1080-1118)

William of Normandy (1028-1087) m. Matilda of Flanders (1031-1083)

47

Family Photographs

Queen Esther Alday Drake circa 1900

John Eager Howard Drake and Queen Esther Alday Drake 1899

John and Esther
circa 1930

John and Esther Drake Family 16 August 1932

front row: Martha Kennedy, William Davis, Charles Tennille,
John (Jackie) Tennille, Clarence Bates holding Clarence Bates,
Jr. \ second row: Della Esther Davis, Queen Esther Drake \
third row: John D. Kennedy, Jr. Held by Johnie Kennedy
(Durward Kennedy behind), Lucius Tennille, John E. Drake, Jr.,
Claudia Tennille, Herbert Drake, John E. Drake, Lillian Bates,
Earnest Davis, Ida Davis.

Queen Esther Alday Drake Funeral Site
and Death Notice

MRS. JOHN E. DRAKE.

BAINBRIDGE, Ga., March 14.—
A funeral service will be held at
the residence this afternoon for Mrs.
John E. Drake, 56, wife of the may-
or of Bainbridge and chairman of
the board of county commissioners.

Mrs. Drake died early Friday
morning after an illness of several
weeks.

Active pall bearers will be Julien
G. Kwilecki, J. B. Gunn, E. F.

Vickers, Byron B. Bower, J. T.
Mitchell, and A. M. Turner, all of
whom are members of the board of
aldermen of Bainbridge. An honor-
ary escort will be composed of
members of the local bar association
and members of the county com-
mission.

Ministers Matthews, Thomson,
Ward, Shell and Scott-Smith will
take part in the service. Interment
will be in Oak City Cemetery.

Survivors include her husband,
who is one of the best known fig-
ures in the life of Bainbridge and
Decatur County; four daughters,
Mrs. Ida Davis, Mrs. L. L. Tennile,
Mrs. Clarence Bates, and Mrs. Dur-
wood Kennedy; two sons, Herbert
Drake and J. E. Drake, Jr.; and
two sisters, Mrs. J. S. Sweet, of
Tampa, Fla., and Mrs. J. G. Thompson, of Blakely.

Acknowledgement

The roots of this project were in old-fashioned hard-copy documents collected by family, supplemented by materials in the genealogical files of the Southwest Georgia Regional Library, in both the Seminole County (Donalsonville) and Decatur County (Bainbridge) collections. When the Alday and Drake families migrated to southwest Georgia in the late eighteenth and early nineteenth centuries that is the area where they settled, and many are still there today.

Of course new technologies and the internet have made genealogical research much easier, while at the same time creating a greater hazzard of error -- error in misinterpreting and choosing among multiple options (a lot of families have many people with the same names; and the same name may show up in multiple, unrelated families) and in errors in entering data onto the web. Still, the dna matching and ease of access to data at Ancestry.com and similar platforms make this kind of research a much more fun, with rewards of personal satisfaction. It is important to note as well that while something is on the internet it isn't necessarily wrong, but it isn't necessarily correct, either. Most of the internet derived data presented here has been verified by comparison with at least one other source.

In all of my writing, I acknowledge the support and assistance from my wife, Harriet, the love of my life and my staunchest critic. She reads, edits, comments and requires me to be sure that the final product says what I want it to say the way I want to say it.   It has been gratifying in this volume to work also with my   daughter, Dr. Robin E. Bates-Murphy, associate professor of English at Lynchburg College, who did the bulk of the research leading to this project.   She took family history from my (inherited) files and further research I had done to assist in editing and expanding my grandfather's memoir, entered that and other research of her own into an Ancestry.com tree, and began to search. With her academic knowledge of Elizabethan English and Irish literature and the knowledge of early English history acquired in her Shakespearean studies she made the connection to names she recognized and connected what started as an Alday family ancestry to the Plantagenets. I have already begun to imagine other projects we might pursue together.   I am a proud papa.

Author Biographies

John W. Bates is Professor Emeritus of Business Administration at Georgia Southwestern State University in Americus, Georgia. A native of Bainbridge, Georgia, Dr. Bates is a graduate of the Georgia Institute of Technology and earned MBA and PH.D. degrees from Georgia State University. He was employed by the State Highway Department of Georgia and the Metropolitan Atlanta Rapid Transit Authority before joining the faculty at Georgia Southwestern. He is an elder in the Presbyterian Church (USA) and completed training for and qualified as a lay pastor in the Flint River Presbytery and the Presbytery of Western North Carolina. He and his wife, Harriet, reside in Hickory, North Carolina.

Robin E. Bates is Associate Professor of English at Lynchburg College, Lynchburg, Virginia. Born in metro Atlanta and raised in Americus, Georgia, she is a graduate of Americus High School, Appalachian State University (B.A. Theater Arts) and earned the M.Ed. from Georgia Southwestern University and Ph.D. from Auburn University. She taught in the English Departments of Auburn and Seton Hall University before moving to Lynchburg, where she and her husband Jonathan Murphy live in a historic home in with their two dogs: Horatio and Imogen.